D0363776

HEROES OF THE WILD WEST

GERONIMO

BY
Jon E. Lewis

This edition first published by Parragon Books in 1995

Produced by
Magpie Books Ltd, London

Copyright © Parragon Book Service Ltd 1995
Unit 13–17, Avonbridge Trading Estate
Atlantic Road
Avonmouth
Bristol BS11 9QD

Cover picture and illustrations courtesy of
Peter Newark's Western Americana

ISBN 0-75250-745-1

A copy of the British Library Cataloguing in Publication
Data is available from the British Library.

Typeset by Hewer Text Composition Services, Edinburgh
Printed in Singapore by Printlink International Co.

HEROES OF THE WILD WEST
Geronimo

Once, when the high summer sun scorched the Sierra Madre, a great war party of Apaches stole down through hidden canyons and across the border into Mexico. Wearing only loin cloths, moccasins on their feet – they were afoot, for this was no time to be encumbered by horses – and bandannas tied around their heads, the Apaches travelled south, covering as much as 40 miles a day. Presently, they reached the town of Arispe, where troops came out to meet them. There were some small skirmishes, but no clear outcome.

The Apaches knew that the next day would bring a big battle, so they allowed Goyahkla ('One Who Yawns') to direct the coming fight. Goyahkla had lost most to the Mexicans – his whole family had been killed by soldiers from this very town – and he had the greatest need for revenge.

Goyahkla arranged his warriors in a crescent in the timber by the river. When, on the following morning, the entire Mexican force – two companies each of infantry and cavalry – marched out, the Apaches waited until the enemy was within the semi-circle and then charged. The Mexicans were sur-rounded, and wild fighting – bayonet against lance, rifle against bow – con-tinued for over two hours.

Goyahkla was everywhere – reckless, almost possessed with blood-lust. Be-cause of his ferocity, Goyahkla was given a new name by the awed and defeated Mexicans, the name of the saint to whom they prayed in their terror. It is the name by which he is still known today.

Geronimo.

The Wars with the Mexicans

The boy who would become Geronimo, slayer of Mexicans and his people's ultimate holdout in their struggle against the United States, was born where the Gila River springs from the earth, in what is now the state of Arizona. Geronimo placed his birth date as June 1829 (although he was almost certainly born several years earlier) and was the fourth of a family of four boys and four girls in the Bedonkohe band of Apaches.

The Dineh (People), as the Apaches referred to themselves, had come to this rocky, arid land long ago, in a time before memory, driving out the Zunis and Comanches to carve a 500-mile range. Here the Apaches lived as nomadic hunters, sheltering against the hostile elements in frail shelters of brush and sticks called wickiups. Although the Apaches were divided into numerous separate bands – Bedonkohe, Chiricahuas, Chihenne, Mimbrenos, Nedni and others – those who trespassed upon their terrain found them a singular and determined antagonist. The name 'Apache' was given them by the Spanish, who heard the Zunis calling them *Apachu*: 'enemy'.

Geronimo, like every Apache male, was trained in the ways of war and hunting almost as soon as he could walk. To develop his endurance and strength he was made to stay awake for days, and go on long cross-country runs. (A mature Apache brave had to be able to walk and run 70 miles a day.) But the training was not only about building brawn; he was also taught to use his brain. For the Apaches, cunning was a greater virtue than anything else, even courage.

Geronimo excelled at this apprenticeship. At the precocious age of seventeen he was admitted to the Council of Warriors, having already participated in four raids – the Apaches, like other Indians, held four as a sacred number – against Mexican caravans and ranches. He had become a man amongst men, and had already reached his adult build:

five feet seven inches in height, big-chested, with a forbidding countenance of overhung brows and a hawk nose. In time, one of his eight battle wounds would cause the right corner of his thin mouth to drop in a permanent sneer.

Perhaps Geronimo's greatest joy in achieving his majority was that he could now marry Alope, a delicate, slender girl of the Nedni tribe with whom he had long been in love. No-po-so, Alope's father, asked a high price of many ponies for his daughter's hand. Undaunted, Geronimo returned a few days later with the necessary number of ponies. He and Alope made their own home, a tepee of buffalo hides furnished with bear and cougar hides. 'We fol-lowed the traditions of our fathers,'

Geronimo said, 'and were happy.' Three children were born to them.

A few years after his marriage – the exact date is uncertain, but some time in 1858 – the Bedonkohe and Mimbrenos Apache bands met in council together to consider their future dealings with the Mexican state of Chihuahua, which lay on the southern fringe of their range. The issue at hand was whether to accept a peace offering. For 200 years the Apaches had preyed upon Chihuahua, and in turn the Mexicans had warred on them. Since 1837, they had even paid bounties for Apache scalps (100 pesos for that of a male Apache, 50 for a woman's, 25 for a child's). Now the state of Chihuahua had decided to try peace with the Apaches. If the Apaches would cease hostilities, the Mexicans would reward them with free blankets and other necessities – including the liquor mescal, for which Apache men had a powerful thirst.

The proposition was tempting. After weighing the dangers against the gains, the great chief of the Mimbrenos, Mangas Coloradas (Red Sleeves), recommended that a party go to Chihuahua to receive the tribute. Most of those gathered agreed with him, including Geronimo, who decided to join the expedition in person. The venture was an important one for his people, and might provide an opportunity to show his leadership capabilities.

It was perhaps only natural that Geronimo felt he had a right to lead.

Chieftainship was hereditary amongst the Apache, and his grandfather had been a chief of the Nedni. However, Geronimo's father had forfeited his – and thus his future son's – inheritance when he joined the Bedonkohe by marriage. The only route to leadership open for Geronimo now was through war. If he proved himself an exceptional warrior, he might win respect eclipsing even that of a hereditary chief.

After a day or so making ready, the expedition – which included women and children, since they would be needed to carry the Mexicans' gifts – left the Apache stronghold of the Mogollon mountains and started south. Their destination, the place where they were to pick up the tribute, was Casa

Grande. On their way, they stopped at Janos, which they knew as Kas–ki–yeh, camping outside the town for several days. During those days, they traded with the people of Janos, who seemed as guileless as the Apaches could have wished.

Late one afternoon, on returning to the camp, Geronimo and other men who had been in the town trading were met by several wailing women. While the men had been away, Mexican soldiers had attacked the camp, slaughtering the guard and many women and children. They had captured all the ponies and supplies.

At this news, the Apaches scattered and hid for the rest of the day, meeting at

Geronimo, leader of the
Chiricahua Apaches.

One of Geronimo's Apache Warriors,
Henry F. Farny.

night to sneak back to the ruined camp.
Geronimo found that his aged mother,
his wife and three small children were
amongst the slain. Only 80 warriors
were left alive, and they had almost no
weapons or ammunition. Mangas
Coloradas decided that retaliation must
wait, and the Apaches returned silently
to their homes in Arizona and New
Mexico.

The murder of his family affected
Geronimo deeply. He gave in to in-
tense grief. Apache custom called for
him to mourn his wife by burning her
tepee, but he went further, destroying all
her belongings, even 'the playthings of
our little ones'. His tribesmen began to
notice a dark change within him. He
became moody and prone to outbursts

of violence. His heart ached for vengeance upon Mexico. His only consolation was that in his grief he received the Power, which visited him when he was weeping alone in the desert. The Power told him that 'No gun can ever kill you'. Henceforth he was invincible.

When the Bedonkohe and their cousins the Mimbrenos were finally ready to take the warpath against the Mexicans, Geronimo was appointed by Mangas Coloradas, then aged 60 but his giant six-foot six-inch body still unstooped by age and his mind as clear as ever, to visit other Apache bands to seek recruits. The commission was a signal honour for a young man of as yet few attainments. Geronimo went first to speak to the Chiricahuas, led by the famous

Cochise. With Cochise's consent, Geronimo addressed the assembled Chiricahuas. 'Kinsmen', he said, according to his later account, 'you have heard what the Mexicans have done without cause. We are men the same as Mexicans are – we can do to them what they have done to us. Let us go forward – we will attack them in their homes. Will you come? It is well – you will all come.'

With the agreement of the Chiricahuas to join the mission, Geronimo next visited the Nedni Apaches and their chief, Juh. They also agreed to participate. The garrison town of Arispe in Sonora was selected as the target.

In the summer of the year following the massacre at Kas-ki-yeh, the warriors of

the four bands held a night-long war
dance around a huge bonfire, moving
out the next day, following secret ways
through the mountains to Arispe. And
there the Apaches fought the pitched
battle which saw Goyahkla become
Geronimo, and the Apaches inflict
upon their old enemy a great and
bloody defeat.

'All the other Apaches were satisfied
after the battle of "Kas-ki-yeh",'
Geronimo said, 'but I still desired more
revenge.' He finally persuaded two other
warriors to join him on some small raids
into Mexico, though they met with little
success in either booty or the killing of
Mexicans. Then, in 1860, he raised a
force of twenty-five men to deal with a
Mexican cavalry company which had

crossed the border to invade the Apache homeland. Geronimo and his warriors ambushed the Mexicans in a mountain defile, wiping them out, but there was little glory in this victory because the Apaches' losses were high. Geronimo himself was wounded in the fight when a Mexican knocked him senseless with a blow from a rifle butt.

Undaunted, Geronimo made another raid into Mexico in the following summer, this time with warriors. They captured a mule train and headed home with it, but were surprised in their camp by a troop of Mexican cavalry. Geronimo was struck near the eye by a bullet, and as he sought cover was hit in the side. They returned home empty-handed. 'Again I was blamed by our people,' said Geronimo, 'and again I had no reply.'

For weeks Geronimo lay in his wickiup waiting for his wounds to heal. One night, while most of the Bedonkohe men were out hunting, three companies of Mexican troops surrounded the village. At daybreak, as the Apache women prepared breakfast, the Mexicans attacked. Many women and children and some warriors were killed. Among the dead was Geronimo's second wife, Nana-tha-thtith, and their child. Those that could fled for their lives into the hills, while the troopers burned their village.

Now Geronimo had the death of another wife and child to avenge. With other Bedonkohe warriors he raided Mexico ceaselessly over the following years, sometimes with conspicuous success. One such raid netted a herd of horses and mules – enough supplies 'to last our whole tribe for a year or more'.

Although Geronimo never rested in his hatred for the Mexicans another, more pressing, problem was beginning to occupy his mind. There were too many White men coming into Arizona.

At War with the White Man

Geronimo saw his first White men, a group of surveyors, in 1858. They were followed by soldiers, and a fort was established. After the soldiers came copperminers, goldminers and silverminers, and soon the Apaches' sacred land was being encroached on all sides. At first the newcomers were warily tolerated, but the fragile peace between the Whites and the People was soon broken. Characteristically, it was the Whites who began the trouble.

General Crook with Apache scouts.

HARPER'S WEEKLY.

JOURNAL OF CIVILIZATION.

Vol. XXX.—No. 1518.

NEW YORK, SATURDAY, JANUARY 9, 1886.

The hunt for Geronimo reaches the news.

In the spring or summer of 1860, Mangas Coloradas went on a friendly visit to the miners at Pinos Altos. The miners tied him to a tree and lashed him unconscious with a bullwhip. The action was as stupid as it was cruel. Mangas Coloradas was the acknowledged chief of the Mimbrenos and the Bedonkohe, who were amongst the most formidable of the fighting Apache. Moreover, he was the father-in-law of the mighty Cochise. Naturally, Mangas Coloradas went on the warpath and, equally naturally, he asked Cochise for aid.

Cochise had his own bitter grievance against the White intruders. In 1861 he had been summoned to a parley with Second Lieutenant George Bascom at Apache Pass. On arrival, he was accused by Bascom of kidnapping a White boy named Ward. Bascom refused to believe his truthful protestations of innocence, and said he intended to take the chief and his family hostage. Cochise escaped only by whipping out his knife, slashing the tent wall and jumping through. The other Indians were held as prisoners. In an effort to free his relatives, Cochise had then captured three White men from a wagon train and offered to exchange prisoners. Bascom had refused, and the affair had ended with Cochise killing his hostages, and Bascom his. As a result of this episode, Cochise wanted to drive the Americans from his land for ever.

Thus the long war against the White man began. Geronimo and the Bedonkohe who followed him placed themselves

under the leadership of Cochise
(Geronimo at this period married She-
gha, a relative of the Cochise family. In
all, Geronimo would marry five times).
The enemy, much to the interest of the
Apache, was divided amongst itself, for
the White man's Civil War had just
begun. In 1862, a column of California
Volunteers for the Union, commanded
by General James Carleton, was detailed
to cross Arizona and take possession of
New Mexico. Their route lay through
Apache Pass.

Alerted by his scouts, Cochise decided
to give the White men a surprise. With
Mangas Coloradas and Geronimo, he
assembled 700 fighting men, the largest
single force the Apaches had ever
wielded in the field. The Indians

mounted an ambush from both sides of the narrow pass, many of the warriors now armed with rifles they had taken from dead 'White-Eyes'.

An advance party of 123 California Volunteers, led by Captain Roberts, entered the Pass on 14 July. The ambush should have been deadly, but Roberts had two mountain howitzers in his train, which he quickly trained on the Apache positions. The Apaches, never having encountered shellfire before, withdrew. It was not to be the Apaches' day. As they retreated, Mangas Coloradas took a severe, although not fatal, bullet wound in the chest.

Less than a year later, Mangas Coloradas, tired of fighting, surrounded by ever more soldiers, decided to take up the White man's offer to talk peace. The old chief, entirely trusting, ventured into Pinos Altos alone, feeling safe because the soldiers were flying a white truce flag. Brevet General Joseph West ordered the chief to be seized, and told his guards, 'I want him dead or alive tomorrow morning. Understand? I want him dead.'

Around the campfire that night the guards heated their bayonets and burned the old chief on his legs and arms. He protested that he was not a child to be played with, whereupon the guards shot him four times. To complete the deed, they scalped and chopped off his head before putting it in a pot to boil. Geronimo characterized the murder of

Mangas Coloradas as 'perhaps the greatest wrong ever done the Indians'.

For ten years after Mangas Coloradas's
death, Cochise fought on against the
White man, his fury only made greater
by this latest betrayal. With the help of
the Warm Springs Apache chiefs
Victorio and Nana – the latter Geronimo's brother-in-law – Cochise fought a
relentless guerrilla war, with small, fast-
moving parties of warriors, often headed
by Geronimo, attacking travellers and
isolated settlements. Never again would
Cochise make the mistake of fighting a
mass, frontal action. The toll Cochise
took was heavy.

But it was not heavy enough. The
White men were too many. 'We kill

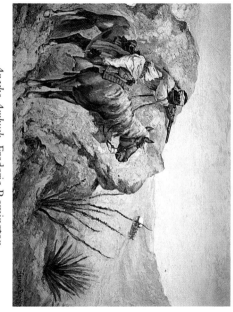

Apache Ambush, Frederic Remington.

Dutchy, an Apache scout of the US Army.

ten; a hundred come in their place', he told his warriors. Cochise, a realist, saw that the struggle against the growing White tide was hopeless. Moreover, he was now an old man. It was time to give up. The other Apache leaders, including Victorio and Nana, already had.

At around the same time that Cochise, with a heavy heart, decided to try the peace path, the US government realized that it needed an Indian policy. Something had to be done about the hostile Indians, especially the Apaches. Washington's approach was two-handed. In 1871, Congress appropriated $70,000 for 'collecting the Apaches of Arizona and New Mexico upon reservations, furnishing them with subsistence and other necessary articles, and to promote peace and civilization among them'. Indians not wishing to partake of this incentive would be dealt with in another way. The same year saw General George Crook, the greatest Indian fighter of the US Army, assigned to Arizona.

Though Crook wanted Cochise for himself, he was obliged to wait upon the peace process. In 1872, President Grant sent pious, one-armed General Oliver O. Howard to talk to the Apaches. Accompanied by mail superintendent Thomas Jeffords, a White man Cochise had befriended after his courage in seeking out the chief to ask him to stop killing his drivers, Howard met Cochise in the mountains, where they spent eleven days in negotiations. Finally, the differences were settled. The

Chiricahuas were allowed to keep their
weapons, and agreed to stay on a reservation set out for them in their beloved
Chiricahua and Dragoon mountains.
Jeffords was to be the reservation
agent, with his agency office near Fort
Bowie. The deal done, Cochise hung up
his war lance. Geronimo, whose Bed-
onkohes had by now been virtually
assimilated into the Chiricahuas, also
entered into the peace agreement. He
even escorted Howard out of the mountains, riding double on the general's
horse, which he mounted in true
Apache style, with a spring over the tail.

For three years, some semblance of
peace descended on the land of the
Apaches. But gradually, impercept-
ibly, things went awry. Cochise died

in 1874, and his son, Taza, if likeable, lacked authority. Larger and larger numbers of Chiricahua warriors came under the influence of Geronimo who, having grown tired of the monotony of reservation life, had adopted his old habit of raiding Mexico. The Mexicans complained bitterly to Jeffords, and in 1876 the Arizonans joined the outcry when two stagecoach attendants and a rancher were killed by drunken Apaches. (The fact that the stagecoach attendants had got the Apaches drunk and tried to cheat them was ignored.) The Governor of Arizona, Anson P. Safford, demanded that Washington replace Jeffords, while Tucson's *Arizona Citizen* declared: 'The kind of war needed for the Chiricahua Apaches is steady, unrelenting, hopeless, and undiscriminating war, slaying men, women and children, until every valley and crest and crag and fastness shall send to high heaven the grateful incense of festering and rotting Chiricahuas.'

The murder of the three White men gave Washington a pretext to close the Chiricahua reservation, something it wanted to do anyway. The year before, in 1875, the Indian Office had adopted a policy of 'consolidation', dissolving the reservations – which only yesterday it had guaranteed the Apaches would last 'forever' – and forcing the inhabitants on to one overcrowded reservation, at San Carlos. Some Apaches refused to go. On learning of the consolidation plan, Geronimo, now aged forty-six, fled across the border to Mexico. His career as a 'renegade' had begun. It would last for eleven years, and become an epic of the American Southwest.

'The Tiger of the Human Race'

Legend has over-simplified Geronimo. He was never a bloodthirsty savage, but nor was he always the principled fighter for the rights of the Apache nation. He was a paradox. The 'tiger of the human race' would sometimes fight, and would sometimes cut and run. He liked music, but thought nothing of killing Mexicans with stones. Even his enemies thought him shrewd, yet he was sometimes prone to indecision. He was never, properly speaking, a chief, although his people considered him a medicine man. No man was more feared by the White-Eyes, even though his followers never numbered more than a hundred.

In one thing he was constant. He desired to be free, to roam and hunt in the wilderness as his ancestors had done before him. Although, under pressure, he would be made to settle on the reservation temporarily, the urge to freedom was always there. But it was not a freedom which could be allowed by the White men, as they 'civilized' the last of the frontier.

Geronimo's first stint as a holdout was inauspicious. Early in 1877 he came out of Mexico, driving a herd of stolen horses, to visit the agency at Warm Springs (Ojo Caliente). The regime at Warm Springs was lax, and the place has used frequently as a refuge by 'renegades' in their cross-border raids. News of Geronimo's whereabouts reached the ears of the Commissioner of Indian Affairs, who wired John Philip Clum, the young (and arrogant) agent of the San Carlos reservation, to arrest Geronimo. Clum immediately set out on the 400-mile journey to Warm Springs, accompanied by about 100 of his Apache Indian police.

After reaching Warm Springs, Clum sent a message to Geronimo and other 'renegade' warriors, who included Chief Victorio, once again on the warpath, that he desired to talk. Having no reason to expect a confrontation, they rode the three miles to the agency accompanied by their wives and children. Geronimo found Clum sitting on the porch of the adobe agency building, a dozen of his police around him. Clum opened the proceedings by accusing Geronimo of killing men and violating the agreement made between Cochise and General Howard. He told Geronimo he was taking him to San Carlos. Geronimo answered defiantly: 'We are not going to San Carlos with you, and unless you are very careful, you and your Apache police will not go back to San Carlos either. Your bodies will stay here at Ojo Caliente to make food for coyotes.' To emphasize

Geronimo (right) and warriors in the Sierra Madre.

Brigadier-General Nelson A. Miles.

the point, Geronimo hitched his rifle up in his arms.

At this moment Clum gave a prearranged signal, a touch of the brim of his hat. The doors of the commissary building burst open and eighty police charged out. Geronimo's thumb began to creep towards the hammer of his rifle, but he thought better of it, and stood stock still instead. Clum stepped forward to disarm the Apache. To the end of his adventurous life – he would be the founder of the *Tombstone Epitaph* and the mayor of that town when it was at its wildest – Clum never forgot the hatred and defiance in Geronimo's face.

This was the only time that Geronimo was ever captured, and then by a trick.

His proud boast to the grave was that the army 'never caught me shooting'.

Conveyed to San Carlos in shackles, Geronimo found the reservation worse than he feared. Situated alongside the Gila River, much of it was low-lying, reaching temperatures of 110 degrees in summer. Rattlesnakes were endemic. The place was wretched.

John Clum who, despite his deceit in the capture of Geronimo, was well-liked by many Apaches, believed he could work with the People and keep them peaceful on the reservation. The army, however, because of the concentration of Apache leaders at San Carlos, sent the cavalry in to guard the reservation. John Clum was forced to disband his self-regulating Apache police. He resigned in protest.

Conditions at San Carlos went from bad to worse. Rations got smaller, due to administrative incompetence and the corruption of civilian contractors, and miners and Mormon farmers began to squat on the Indians' best land. There were outbreaks of malaria and smallpox.

Victorio fled almost immediately, moving back with his people to Warm Springs. The army refused to leave them in peace. Victorio declared he would 'make war forever' against the USA. He was killed in 1880 in a fight with Mexican soldiers.

Geronimo endured the reservation for a year. He had little choice, for much of the time he was imprisoned, an experience he thought 'might easily have been death to me'. As soon as he was able he escaped to Mexico with a few other Chiricahuas. He returned voluntarily in 1880, following a bitter winter of starvation in the mountains, but again did not stay long.

His next breakout was occasioned by more than a desire to walk the mountains in freedom. During the spring of 1881, a religious movement arose among the reservation Apache which preached the end of the white man and the rising again of the old Apache order. In August, the agent sent a detachment of soldiers to arrest the spiritual leader of the movement, Noch–ay–del–klinne. His followers

Frederic Remington illustration of a
wounded cavalry soldier.

Chato, the Chiricahua chief who became
an army scout.

attacked the troops and a pitched battle ensued, with dead on both sides. Army reinforcements were rushed in, and the rumour began to circulate that the Apache leaders would be arrested. More specifically, the rumours said that Geronimo – who had evidenced a hard-headed scepticism about the new religion – was to be hanged. In September of 1881, in response to these rumours, Geronimo and the Nedni chief, Juh, along with seventy warriors, jumped the reservation and made for the Sierra Madre. Their route took them past Tombstone, where a posse including three of the famous Earp brothers tried to head them off, to no avail. Geronimo was free once more.

Six months later (April 1882), Geronimo and his band returned to the reservation but not, this time, as captives. They rode in, with an audacity that caused even 'injun'-haters to marvel, as liberators. They persuaded most of the remaining Chiricahuas and Warm Springs Apaches to leave with them for Mexico. Near the border, at Horse Shoe Canyon, pursuing cavalry caught up with them. The warriors fought a brilliant rearguard action, allowing the main body of women and children to cross into Mexico. Then disaster struck from an unexpected source. A Mexican infantry regiment stumbled upon the Apaches, killing most of the women and children who were riding in front.

Among the warriors and chiefs who managed to escape were Naiche (a son of Cochise) Loco, Chato, and Geronimo himself. Embittered, they joined up with old Nana, chief of the Mimbrenos after the death of Victorio, to form a united guerrilla band of eighty warriors.

Over the next two years, Geronimo and the other 'renegades' attacked Mexican towns and villages, invariably beating the superior Mexican forces sent out to deal with them. More than once, Geronimo's Power alerted them to unseen dangers, so helping them avoid Mexican ambushes. Periodically, the Apache fighters recrossed the border to raid American settlements and ranches, becoming more daring all the time.

To stop the outrages, the Army again called on George Crook, who had been sent north from Arizona some years before to fight the Sioux and Cheyenne. His experiences there had changed 'Gray Wolf', as the Indians called him. He no longer regarded them as vermin, but as human beings. On 4 September 1882 Crook assumed command at San Carlos and, on talking to the Apaches on the reservation, found that their grievances were justified. The reservation Apaches, he concluded, 'had not only the best reasons for complaining, but had displayed remarkable forbearance in remaining at peace'. He began a reform of the corrupt practices of White contractors and suppliers and set about re-establishing John Clum's Apache Police.

Crook also gave much thought to the band of Apaches free in Mexico. He did not want another guerrilla war with the Apaches, and knew that it was almost impossible to defeat them in the rugged country they called home. Crook decided that he should meet with Geronimo and the other leaders, and that the best place to do this was in Mexico. But in order to cross the border, he had to wait for the Apaches to make a raid in the USA. By international agreement, he could go into Mexico only in pursuit of renegade Apaches. Then came his lucky break.

On 21 March 1883, a renegade Apache war party raided a mining camp near Tombstone. A few days later the same raiders killed federal judge H. C. McComas and his wife, and abducted their son. It was the excuse Crook needed, and with a force of fifty soldiers and 193 civilian Apache scouts – Crook firmly believed that you needed an Apache to catch an Apache – he went into Mexico. After searching for several weeks, the scouts located Geronimo's camp and captured the women and children. Geronimo, by now, was the undisputed leader of the holdout Apaches, and the men were out on a raid of a Mexican ranch. The capture of the camp was a stunning blow to Geronimo, for he had thought himself virtually invulnerable in the fastness of the Mexican mountains. Crook sent him a message indicating that he wanted to talk. Geronimo stayed away on a mountain top. It was only when Crook, in one of the most courageous acts of his career,

Harper's Weekly illustration of an Apache horse-stealing raid.

Geronimo in 1900.

walked up alone to meet him and the other hostile leaders that parleying began.

Geronimo and Crook talked for three days, and the Apache found Crook to be surprisingly generous. When Crook agreed that Geronimo and the others had been badly treated at San Carlos, and when he said he did not intend to take away their weapons, Geronimo agreed to return. However, Geronimo added that it would take him two months to round up all the Chirica-huas. To Geronimo's surprise Crook agreed.

True to his word, Geronimo crossed the border voluntarily, although he stretched the two months to eight, arriving in February of 1884. Before him he drove 350 head of cattle, stolen from the Mexicans. This seemed quite proper to Geronimo, who felt he was only supplying his people with meat. At San Carlos, Crook took a different view and confiscated the herd, ordered it sold and returned the proceeds to the original Mexican owners.

For more than a year things were quiet on the reservation, and Crook could proudly say that 'not an outrage or depredation of any kind' was committed by the Apaches. Outside San Carlos, however, the White citizens of Arizona were stirring up trouble. Newspapers contained all sorts of lurid fabricated stories about atrocities committed by Geronimo and called upon vigilantes to hang him. There was much criticism of Crook for being too easy on the Apaches; some even suggested that he had surrendered to Geronimo in Mexico, and was now providing him with an easy life in return for the keeping of his scalp.

The stories reached Geronimo's ears and made him uneasy. He also feared trouble from the reservation authorities for breaking the rule that prohibited the drinking of tiswin (corn beer), a pleasure the Apaches found themselves unable to resist. Expecting the worst, Geronimo, Nana and ninety-two women and children, eight boys and thirty-four men departed for Mexico on the night of 17 May 1885. Before leaving, Geronimo cut the telegraph wire.

Geronimo's flight was the signal for hysteria in the Arizonan newspapers. Headlines read 'THE APACHES ARE OUT!', and there was much baying for Indian blood. Meanwhile, Geronimo himself was trying to avoid any confrontation with the Whites, and was hurrying his people towards Mexico, not even stopping to make camp. Eventually, they made the safety of the familiar Sierra Madre.

Once again, General Crook was detailed by Washington to apprehend the fugitive Geronimo. Crook was either to take the Apache's unconditional surrender or kill him. To fulfil his mission, Crook mounted the heaviest campaign in the Apache wars up to that time, with more than 2,500 cavalry troopers and 200

Indian scouts. (Some of these were old Apache cohorts of Geronimo, including Chato; the Apaches, understanding the boredom of reservation life, did not usually blame People who scouted for the Whites.)

Throughout the winter of 1885–6, Crook hunted his foe in the Sierra Madre, but having been surprised there once Geronimo was more cautious. In January 1886, Crook's force managed to discover and attack one renegade camp, although their quarry got away. But in March, Geronimo decided to surrender. Units of the Mexican Army, as well as the US cavalry, were combing the Sierra Madre for him. Caught between the Mexicans who only wanted to kill him, and the Americans who only wanted to capture him, Geronimo opted to meet with Crook at Cañon de los Embudos (Canyon of Tricksters), a few miles south of the border.

When the general arrived at the meeting place, he did not find Geronimo or his men looking particularly discouraged. 'Though tired of the constant hounding of the campaign', Crook later recalled, 'they were in superb physical condition, armed to the teeth, fierce as so many tigers. Knowing what pitiless brutes they are themselves, they mistrust everyone else.'

He and Geronimo talked for two days, and Geronimo agreed once more to live on the reservation. 'Do with me what

Poster for a Wild West show featuring Geronimo.

Geronimo (in top hat) at the St Louis World's Fair.

you please', he said. 'Once I moved about like the wind. Now I surrender to you, and that is all.'

The Apache wars seemed to be over. The peace, however, proved short-lived.

Surrender

Despite his submission to Crook, within days Geronimo had gone fugitive. On the dark and rainy night of 28 March, as he and his surrendered Chiricahua band neared Fort Bowie, Geronimo, his young son Chappo, Naiche and seventeen other warriors, along with eighteen women and children, slipped away from their escort. 'I feared treachery', he later said, 'and decided to remain in Mexico.' A trader had got the hostiles drunk and filled them full of tales about how the local people were going to make 'good injun' of them. It would be Geronimo's last break-out.

As a result of Geronimo's flight, the War Department severely reprimanded Crook for laxity and his over-indulgences towards the Indians. Crook resigned immediately, and was replaced by Brigadier-General Nelson A. Miles, whose orders were to 'capture or destroy' Geronimo and his coterie of hostiles. Strictly speaking, Miles managed to do neither, although his work amongst the Apaches would prove destructive enough. One of his first decisions was to transfer all the Mimbrenos and Chiricahuas on the reservations – including the scouts who had helped Crook – to Florida.

For the manhunt of Geronimo, Miles put 5,000 soldiers – a quarter of the entire army – in the field, and built 30 heliograph stations to flash messages from mountain to mountain, a system of communication well known to the Apaches, who had long since shifted from smoke signals to mirrors. Meanwhile, Geronimo raided almost at will. In April of 1886, he and his warriors crossed into Arizona and killed a rancher's wife, child and an employee. A short while later, Geronimo's war party killed two men outside of Nogales, and then ambushed the cavalry sent in pursuit of them. Two troopers died. The Apaches suffered not a single loss. Geronimo would later say of this period: 'We were reckless of our lives, because we felt that everyman's hand

Apache Indian country, Arizona.

Modern-day Apaches perform a traditional devil dance.

was against us. If we returned to the reservation we would be put in prison and killed; if we stayed in Mexico they would continue to send soldiers to fight us; so we gave no quarter to anyone and asked no favours.'

Throughout the summer of 1886, Miles pursued Geronimo and his 'army' of twenty warriors, to no avail. They seemed as elusive as ghosts. Finally, Miles decided to try another tack – he would negotiate with the enemy. His appointed emissary was Lieutenant Charles Gatewood, who knew the ways of the Apaches well and had met Geronimo himself a number of times. Accompanying Gatewood were two scouts, Martine and Kayitah.

To make contact with the renegades, Gatewood headed across the border and simply roamed around, listening for word of the Apaches' whereabouts. Eventually, he discovered that Geronimo was sending women into the small town of Fronteras to procure mescal. He trailed one such woman out of Fronteras and deep into the Sierra Madre. It was the end of August 1886.

Watching Gatewood's scouts make their way up the canyon towards his *rancheria*, Geronimo ordered them to be shot. Some of his warriors protested that they were brave men to risk such a venture. Grudgingly, Geronimo assented that they could live, and had them escorted into camp. He kept one scout as hostage,

and sent the other back to Gatewood
with a message that he would hear what
Gatewood had to say. The next day,
Gatewood met the hostiles at the desig-
nated meeting place, a bend by the river.
Geronimo calmly laid down his rifle and
walked over to Gatewood (Big Nose, to
the Apaches), shook his hand and asked
how he was. But when they sat down to
talk and smoke cigarettes in the Apache
fashion, with tobacco rolled in oak
leaves, Geronimo deliberately sat so
close to the lieutenant that he could
feel his revolver.

Geronimo opened the council formally
by announcing that he and his warriors
had come to hear General Miles's message. Gatewood gave it to them straight.
'Surrender, and you will be sent to join

the rest of your friends in Florida, there to await the decision of the President as to your final disposition. Accept these terms or fight it out to the bitter end.' At this Geronimo bristled, 'Take us to the reservation (San Carlos), or fight!'

Gatewood then had to inform Geronimo that the reservation no longer existed, and that all the Chiricahuas had been removed to Florida, including members of Geronimo's own family.

The news was a real blow to the renegades. Geronimo asked about Bear Coat Miles. Could he be trusted? Was his voice harsh or agreeable? Did he look you in the eyes when he talked? Then he said to Gatewood: 'We want your advice. Consider yourself one of us and not a White man. Remember all that has been said today, and as an Apache, what would you advise us to do under the circumstances?'

'I would trust General Miles and take him at his word', Gatewood replied.

The Indians withdrew for a private council, which in the Apache way was democratic, with everyone having a voice, although Geronimo as leader had much influence. Perico, Fun, Ahnandia – all of them Geronimo's cousins – indicated that they wished to surrender so that they might see their loved ones again. Although Geronimo still had a taste to fight on until the mortal end, he was weakened by these defections. He stood for a few moments without speaking. At length he said, 'I have been depending heavily on you three men. You have been great fighters in battle. If you are going to surrender, there is no use my going without you. I will give up with you.'

And so Geronimo, the last of the Apache leaders, surrendered for the final time.

In Captivity

After his surrender, Geronimo was escorted to meet General Miles at Skeleton Canyon for a formal cessation of hostilities. When the general failed to get to the meeting on time the wary Geronimo very nearly fled once more, even trying to talk Gatewood into joining him.

Miles finally arrived on 3 September, and Geronimo went forward to meet him. 'General Miles is your friend,' the interpreter told the Apache leader.

'I never saw him, but I have been in need of friends', said Geronimo. 'Why has he not been with me?'

When this was interpreted, laughter broke out amongst those present.

The general, who assured the fugitives that they would soon see their families in Florida, was impressed by this wild antagonist. As the general saw him: 'He was one of the brightest, most resolute, determined looking men that I have ever encountered. He had the clearest, sharpest dark eye I think I have ever seen, unless it was that of General Sherman when he was at the prime of life . . . Every movement indicated power, energy and determination. In everything he did, he had a purpose.'

Geronimo's purpose now was surrender. The ceremony was officially concluded on the afternoon of 4 September. The following day Miles flashed the news to a grateful White nation that Geronimo had finally given up arms.

With a last farewell glimpse at the Chiricahua mountains, Geronimo was taken to Fort Bowie, and from there transported, along with his hostile band, in a railway cattle car to San Antonio, Texas. The newspapers were as full as ever with horror stories about Geronimo's 'depredations', and the Apache only just escaped being tried by a civilian court in the town. (Among those who wanted to see Geronimo hung high was the 'Great Father' in Washington, President Grover Cleveland.) From San Antonio, Geronimo was shipped to Fort Pickens in Florida, a crumbling, abandoned fortification on Santa Rosa island. It was the start of twenty-three years of captivity.

Probably Geronimo was not surprised, after all these years of dealing with the White man, to find that he had been lied to one more time. He did not, as General Miles had promised him, see his family on arrival in Florida, and instead spent two years in close confinement. To the great distress of Geronimo and the other male hostiles, the women and children of their band were taken from them and sent to Fort Marion, 300 miles across the state.

The warm and humid land of Florida, so unlike the dry country of Arizona and New Mexico, was not healthy for the Apaches. More than a hundred died of a disease diagnosed as consumption. Their children were sent away to a school in Carlisle, Pennsylvania, where they were to be prepared for integration into White man's society. 'Our job', said the school's founder, is to 'kill the Indian and save the man'.

After two years of misery in Florida, the hostile warriors were transferred to Mount Vernon Barracks in Alabama. To their great joy, there they were finally reunited with their families, with

Geronimo seeing an infant daughter Lenna for the first time. To those accustomed to seeing the Apache warlord as an 'inhuman monster', the care he showed for his daughter was striking. One visitor wrote: 'I had luck today . . . Saw Geronimo . . . He is a terrible old villain, yet seemed quiet enough today nursing a baby.' Aside from family reunions, the pleasures to be found at Mount Vernon were few. The Apaches were put to work at hard labour. Their rations were pitiful. There were several outbreaks of tuberculosis and pneumonia. Many became depressed. Nineteen of the 352 Chiricahua prisoners died within eight months.

If it had not been for the efforts of a few White friends of the Apaches such as

John Clum and George Crook, many more would have died at the barracks on the Mobile River. In August 1894 the War Department was finally persuaded to move the Apaches back west, although not as far as their original stomping grounds. They were sent to Fort Sill, in southern Oklahoma, which their old enemies, the Comanches and Cheyenne, generously offered to share with them. Here the White men set about turning the wild Apaches into brown copies of themselves. They were given small log houses, made to learn handiwork, made to garden, growing melons and cantaloupes on small patches of land, and made to farm. At one point, Geronimo was forced to learn how to be a cowboy. The Apaches, in fact, did well at raising cattle, but only moderately well at the other trades.

The one thing at which Geronimo excelled in captivity was selling himself. The Apache had always had a hard head for business, and he was soon making and purveying Geronimo souvenirs for the steady stream of visitors who dropped by to view him. One such visitor wrote, in a lively sketch of Geronimo the businessman:

'Geronimo has an eye to thrift and can drive a sharp bargain with his bows and arrows, and quivers and canes, and other work, in which he is skillful. He prides himself upon his autograph, written thus, GER-ONIMO, which he affixes to what he sells, usually asking an extra price for it. He had a curious headdress, which he called . . . his war bonnet . . . He seemed to value this bonnet highly, but finally in his need or greed for money, offered it for sale for $25.'

In 1898, Geronimo met up with General Miles at the Trans-Mississippi Exposition in Omaha, where the old warrior was the prime exhibit. He asked the former clerk to use his influence to allow him to return to Arizona. 'The acorns and piñon nuts, the quail and the wild turkey, the giant cactus and the palo verdes – they all miss me', said Geronimo. 'A very beautiful thought, Geronimo', laughed Miles. 'Quite poetic. But the men and women who live in Arizona, they do not miss you.

Folks in Arizona sleep now at night. They have no fear that Geronimo will come and kill them. The acorns and the piñon nuts will have to get along as best they can without you.'

Later that year Miles visited Geronimo at Fort Sill. The army man again told Geronimo that he would not be allowed home. However, he did agree to Geronimo's request that he might be excused from forced labour because of his age. He was sixty-nine years old. From then on, the Apache worked only when he felt like it. The old warrior also converted to Christianity, and joined the Dutch Reformed Church in 1903. But he was not a member of the congregation for long; he was expelled within months for his inveterate gambling.

In 1904, Geronimo was invited to take part in the St Louis World's Fair. He took a ride on the Ferris wheel, and had his picture taken in an automobile. 'I am glad I went to the Fair', he said afterwards. 'I saw many interesting things and learned much of the White people.' The trip was profitable in more tangible ways too. He sold signed photographs of himself, and returned with more money than he had ever had before.

The next year he was taken to Washington to ride in Theodore Roosevelt's inaugural parade. This was also good business. People bought his autographs for 25 cents as quickly as he could write them. Geronimo stole the show. Only the president himself attracted more attention.

When the parade was over, Geronimo was able to meet Roosevelt. He took advantage of the occasion to plead for a return to Arizona:

'Great Father, other Indians have homes where they can live and be happy. I and my people have no homes. The place where we are kept is bad for us . . . We are sick there and we die. White men are in the country that was my home. I pray you to tell them to go away and let my people go there and be happy.

'Great Father, my hands are tied as with a rope. My heart is no longer bad. I will tell my people to obey no chief but the Great White

Chief. I pray you to cut the ropes and make me free. Let me die in my own country, an old man who has been punished enough.'

Roosevelt was sympathetic, but his reply was essentially the same as Miles's. The people of Arizona would not stand for it. He told Geronimo, 'I am sorry, and have no feeling against you.'

In the autumn of the same year, Mr S. M. Barrett, the White Superintendent of Education in Lawton, Oklahoma, secured permission from Roosevelt to interview Geronimo about his life. Geronimo related the tale in the Apache language to Asa Daklugie, the son of Juh, who translated it into English for Barrett to write down. More than anything in his old age Geronimo wanted to be allowed to return to the land of the Chiricahuas, and in telling his life story he diplomatically left out most of his dealings with Americans. The book, *Geronimo's Story of His Life*, was dedicated to President Roosevelt.

By now Geronimo's years were piling up, and his rugged, squat body was showing signs of wear. Yet it took an accident to kill him. On a cold night in February 1909 he fell, drunk, off his horse and lay in a freezing creek all night. He developed severe pneumonia. He fought the illness for seven days, but it eventually overwhelmed him. Geronimo died at 6.15 in the morning of 17 February, and was buried the following day in Fort Sill's cemetery. He was about eighty years old, and still technically a prisoner of war.

He was never to realize his dream of returning to Arizona. But there was one thing nobody could ever wrest from him – the memory of freedom. And the knowledge that it had taken 5,000 Whites, and a series of false promises, finally to subdue his thirty-eight Apaches.

There was a small triumph at the end, too. When his family came to divide his possessions they discovered that his souvenir business had been very lucrative indeed. The old warrior had made a tidy pile of money off the Palefaces.